A ROOKIE READER®

WHERE'S BROOKE?

By Ellen Javernick

Illustrated by Rick Hackney

Prepared under the direction of Robert Hillerich, Ph.D.

CHILDRENS PRESS®
CHICAGO

Library of Congress Cataloging-in-Publication Data

Javernick, Ellen.
    Where's Brooke? / by Ellen Javernick ; illustrated by
Richard Hackney.
        p.   cm. — (A Rookie reader)
    Summary: As a father looks all over for his young
daughter, the reader can see her close by him all the
time.
   ISBN 0-516-02012-9
    [1. Fathers and daughters—Fiction. 2. Stories in
rhyme.] I. Hackney, Rick, ill. II. Title. III. Series.
PZ8.3.J36   1992
[E]—dc20   92-11097
                                          CIP
                                          AC

"Where's Brooke?
Is she there on
the chair?"

3

"No, that's just her bear."

"In back of the clock?"

5

"It's only a sock."

6

"Could she be in her bed?"

8

"Her hair is not red."

9

"Where's Brooke?"

11

"Did she hide?

I'll look inside."

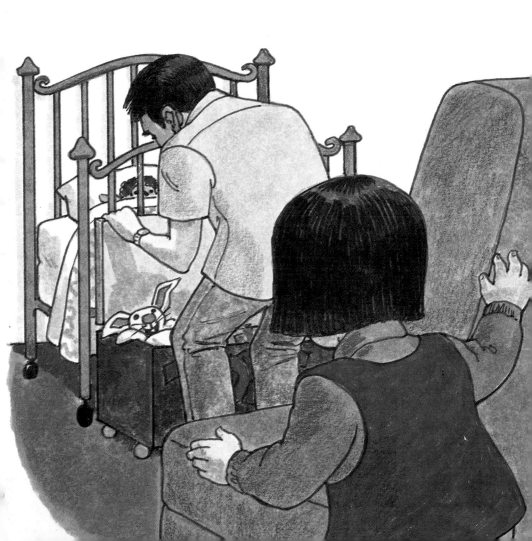

"But I did hear a sound.
She must be around."

"Where's Brooke?"

19

"Behind the door?

No. I'll have to look more."

"Are you there, Brooke dear?"

"She's not under here."

24

"I'm very, very certain,
She's not behind that curtain."

28

"I guess I'll go away.
Brooke must not want to play."

"Look, Dad, look.
Here's Brooke."

WORD LIST

			it's	she
a	certain	hall	just	she's
all	chair	have	look	sock
are	clock	hear	more	sound
around	could	her	must	that
at	curtain	here	no	that's
away	Dad	here's	not	the
back	dear	hide	of	there
be	did	I	on	to
bear	don't	I'll	only	under
bed	door	I'm	out	very
behind	go	in	play	want
Brooke	guess	inside	red	where's
but	hair	is	see	you

About the Author

Ellen Javernick is a preschool and kindergarten teacher in Loveland, Colorado. She has an M.A. in early childhood education and is active in professional organizations. An experienced freelance writer with hundreds of magazine articles to her credit, she is the author of *What If Everybody Did That?* published by Childrens Press. Also, Mrs. Javernick has written *Celebrate the Christian Family* and two other books for teachers.

Mrs. Javernick and her husband, Frank, have five children: Mike, Becky, Andy, Matt, and Lisa.

About the Artist

Richard Hackney is a San Francisco illustrator and writer who graduated from Art Center School in Los Angeles, California. He has worked at Disney Studios, drawn a syndicated comic strip, and has been an art director in advertising. He has also done some acting, written children's stories, and currently is doing a lot of educational illustration.

Richard lives with his wife, Elizabeth, and a black cat in a home on the edge of San Francisco Bay.